Before drawing the contours of the browline, nose, lips, and chin, draw an oval for the face with a line across the center for the eyes first to situate the facial elements accurately.

Leonardo da Vinci
(1452–1519)
FIVE STUDIES OF GROTESQUE FACES
15TH CENTURY
Red chalk on paper
Photo Scala, Florence, courtesy of the Ministero Beni e Attività Culturali

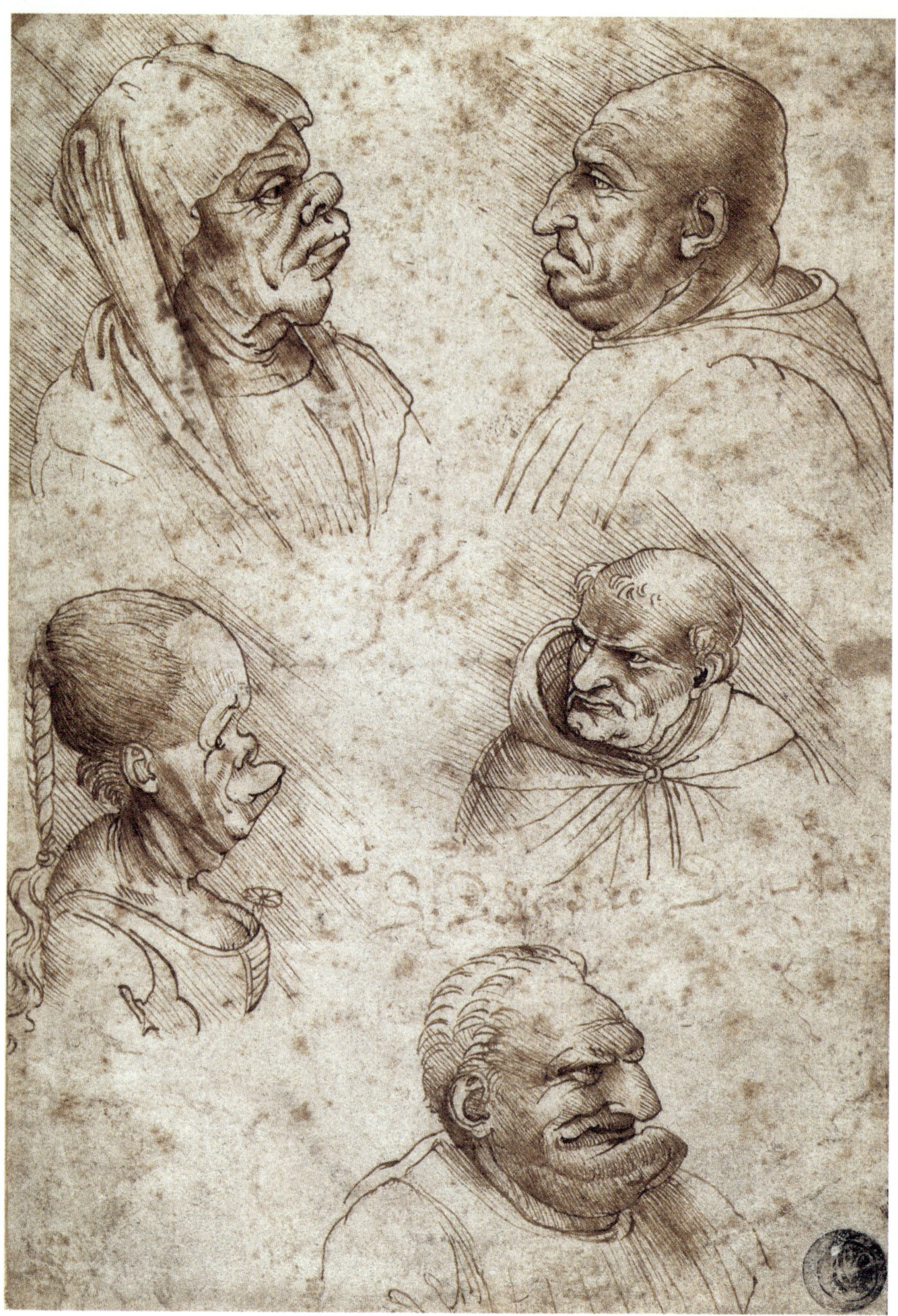

Da Vinci's caricatures are presented here as quick studies using rudimentary hatching—a method of conveying three-dimensionality and shadow. The hatching lines run downward from left to right, a characteristic often identified with left-handed artists such as da Vinci.

Pay attention to people in the streets and piazze and fields, and note them down with a brief indication of the forms; thus for a head make an O, and for an arm a straight or a bent line, and the same for the legs and the body, and when you return home work out these notes in complete form.

LEONARDO DA VINCI

Far more than just through different skin tones, think about how you might represent race and background in a portrait. By close observation, you will be able to pick up on the small physical differences and proportions individual to each person.

It is the actual act of drawing that forces the artist to look at the object in front of him, to dissect it in his mind's eye and put it together again.

JOHN BERGER

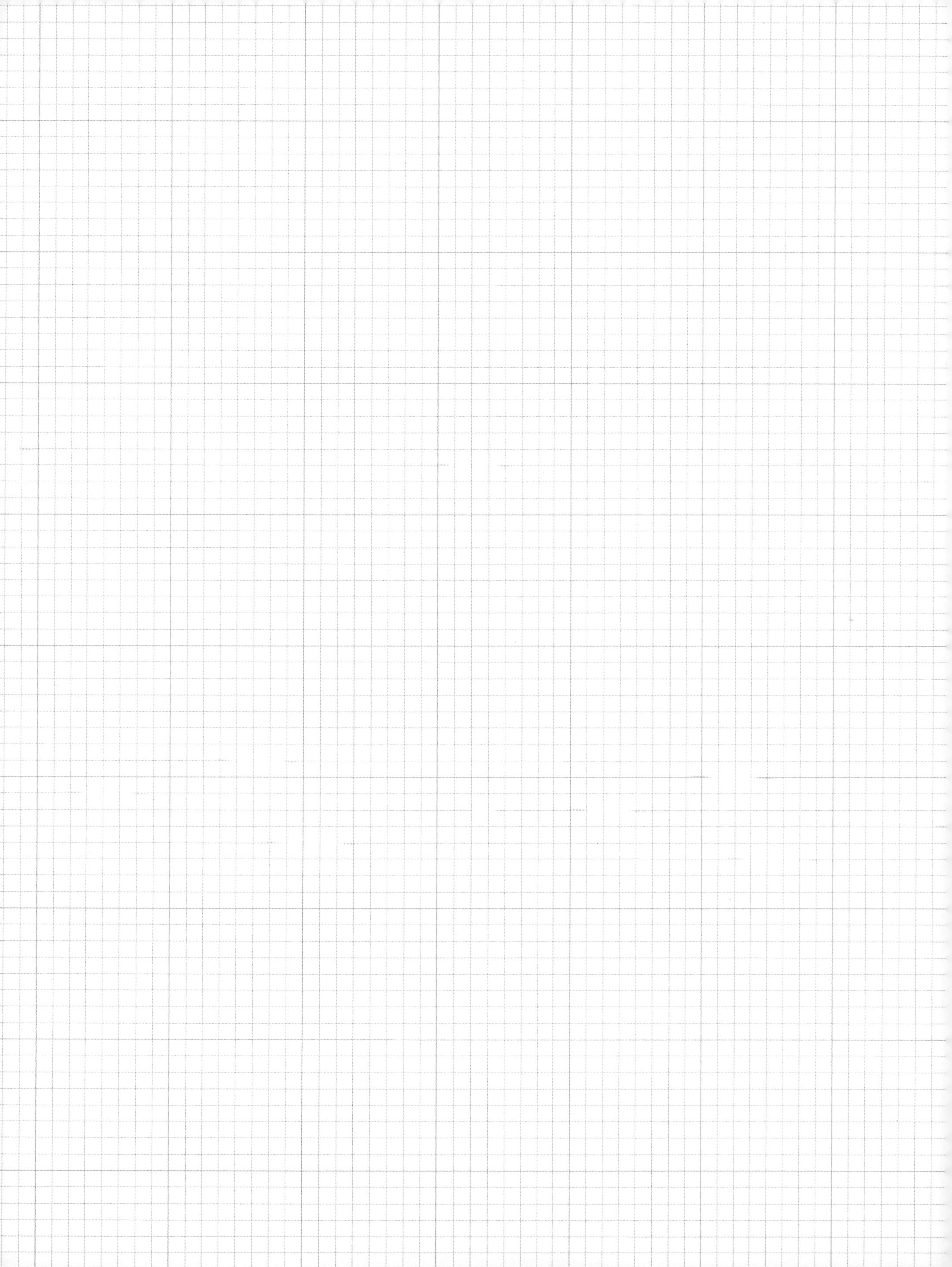

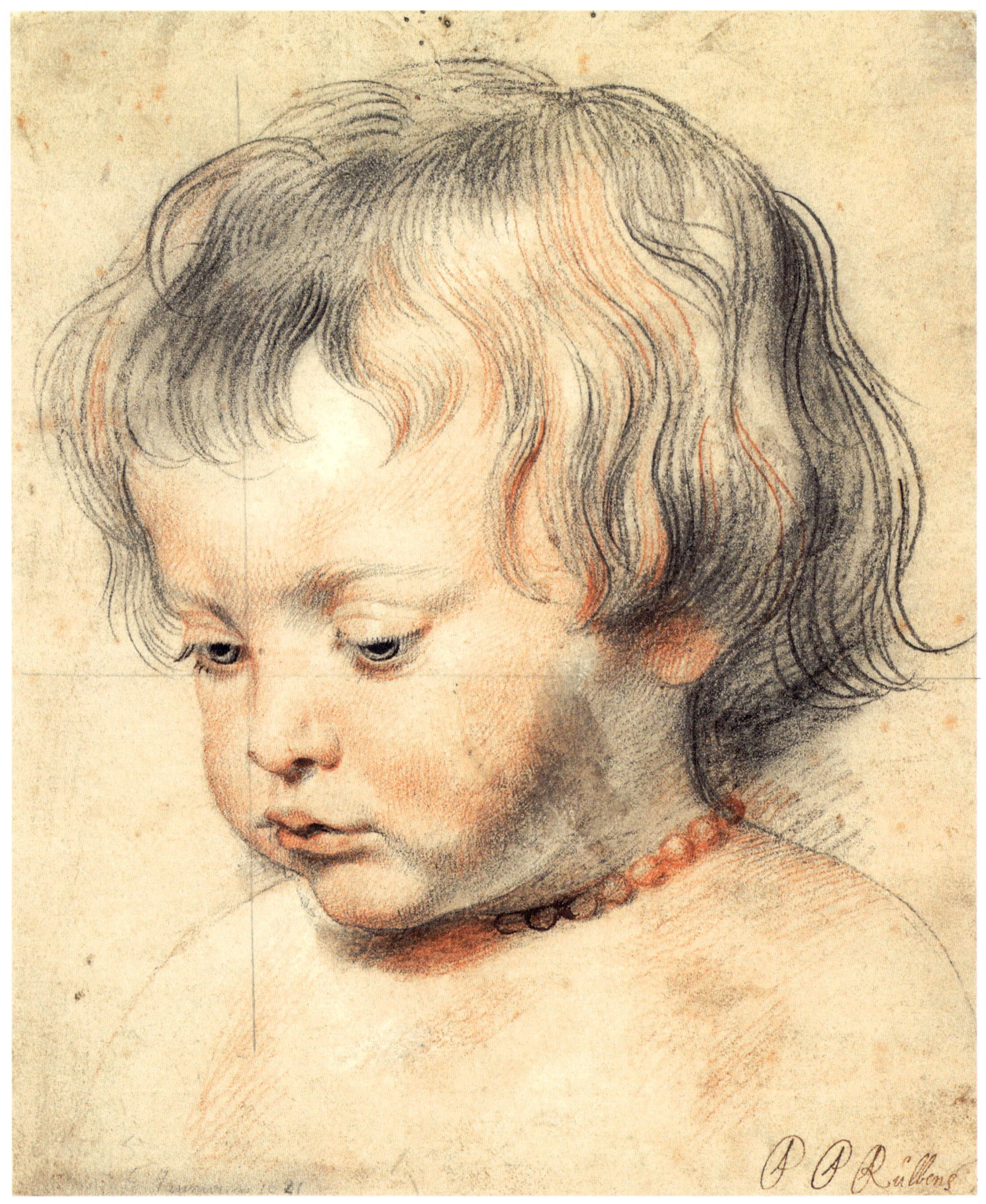

Peter Paul Rubens
(1577–1640)
NICOLAAS RUBENS WEARING A CORAL NECKLACE
C.1619
Black and red chalk, accented with white chalk
Heritage Image Partnership/ Alamy Stock Photo

Judging from this and other drawings of his children, Rubens must have adored them and drawn them repeatedly, often while they were absorbed in other things . . . He recorded them swiftly, sketching in black chalk with touches of red chalk for their faces.

ANNE-MARIE LOGAN AND MICHIEL C. PLOMP

Brown paper represents the primal twilight of the first toil of creation, and with a bright-colored chalk or two you can pick out points of fire in it, sparks of gold, and blood-red, and sea-green, like the first fierce stars that sprang out of divine darkness.

G. K. CHESTERTON

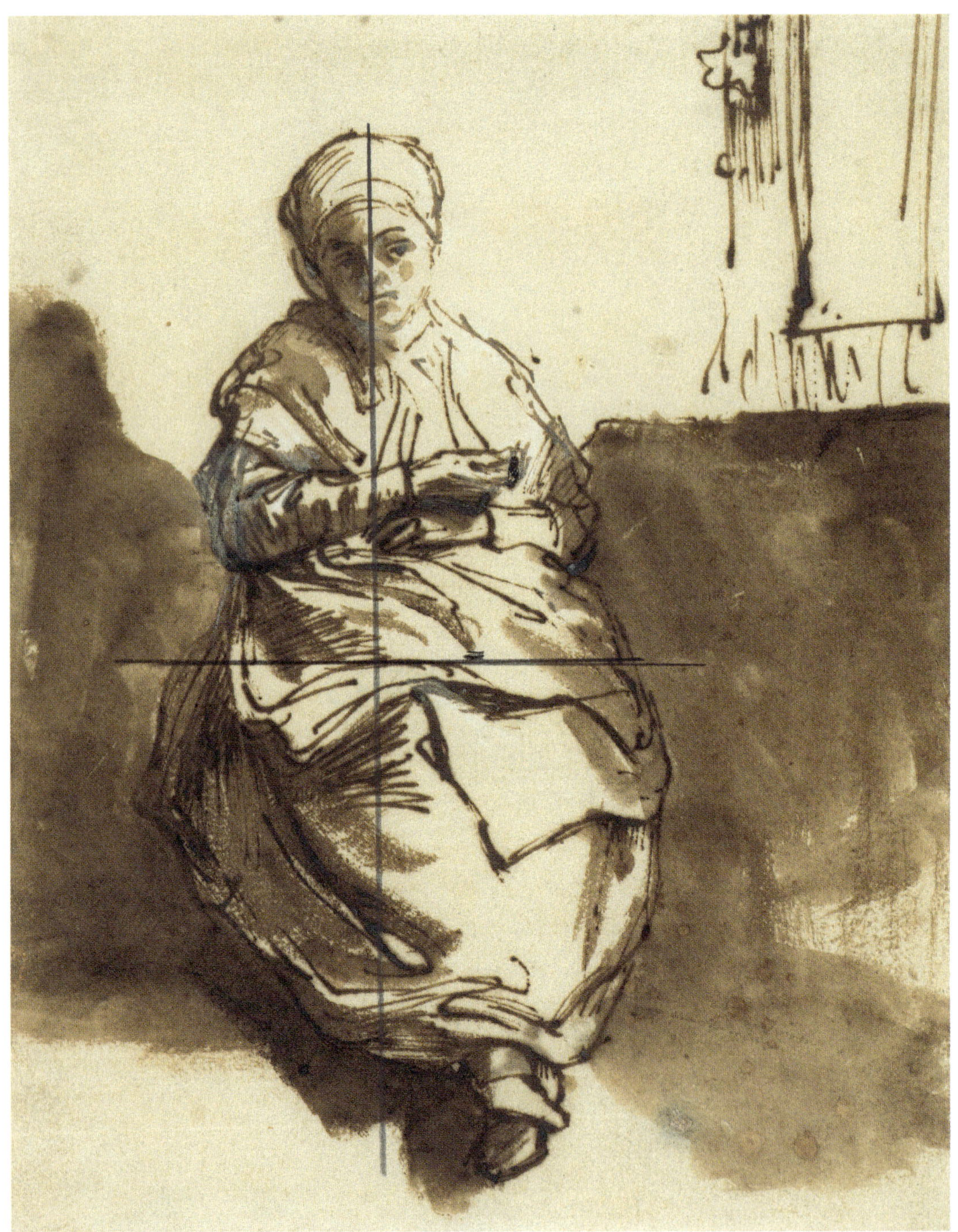

Rembrandt van Rijn
(1606–69)
YOUNG WOMAN (SASKIA) SITTING BY THE WINDOW
1636–40
Pen and brush in brown, corrections with white
Rijksmuseum, Amsterdam

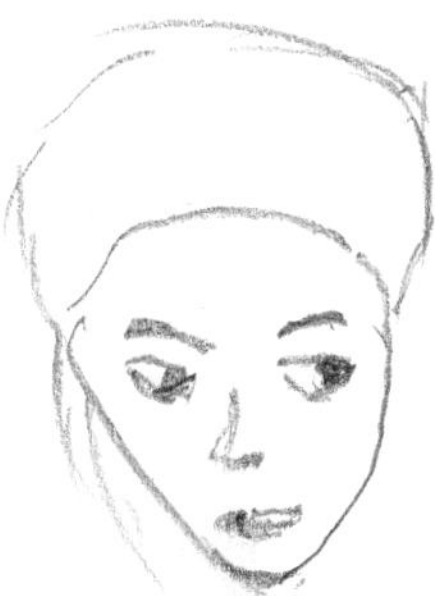

Rembrandt put more in the face than anyone else ever has, before or since, because he saw more . . . His work is a great example of the hand, the eye—and the heart.

DAVID HOCKNEY

Try to put well in practice what you already know; and in so doing, you will in good time, discover the hidden things which you now inquire about.

REMBRANDT VAN RIJN

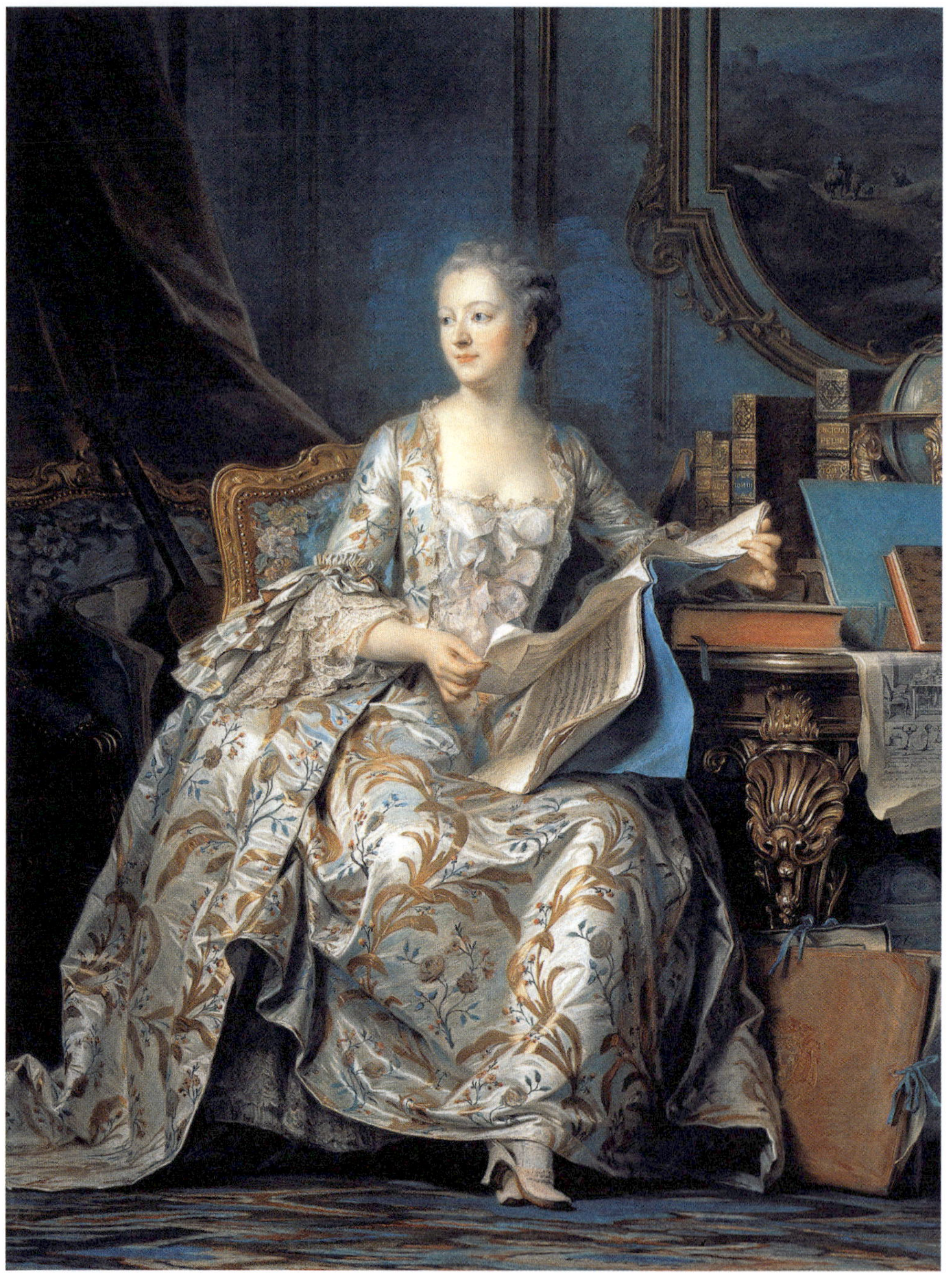

Maurice-Quentin de La Tour
(1704–88)
JEANNE POISSON (1721–64) THE MARQUISE DE POMPADOUR, 1755
Pastel on paper mounted on canvas
Louvre, Paris/ Bridgeman Images

Pompadour was the official mistress of Louis XV and a great patron of the arts. While communicating power and wealth with her ostentatious clothes and furniture, the portrait is also intimate: the marquise sits in her own home, surrounded by evidence of causes close to her heart.

During the period of La Tour's work here, commissioned portraits were used to assert the sitter's role. Consider props when arranging your composition. What might they say about your sitter?

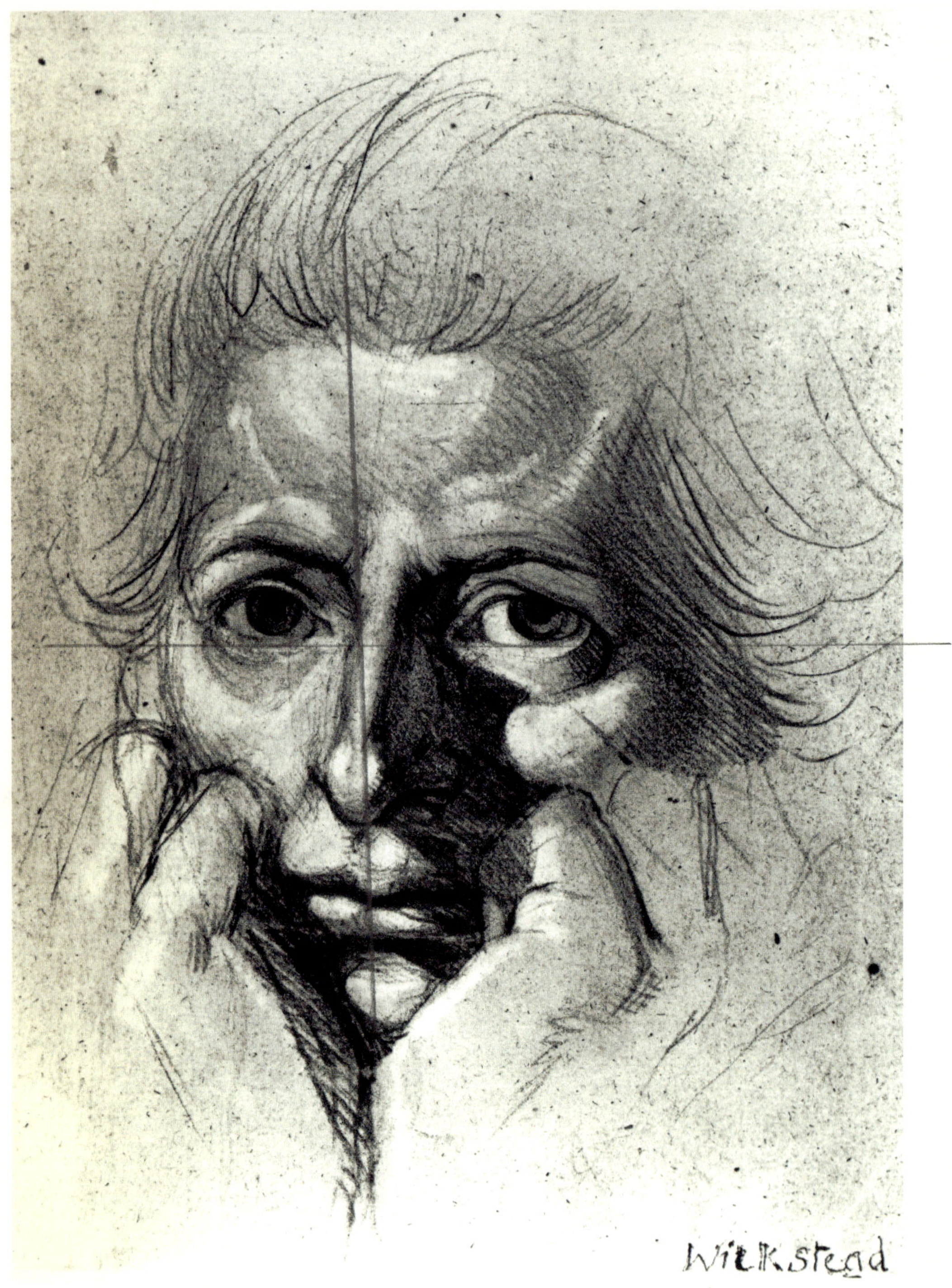

Henry Fuseli
(1741–1825)
STUDY FOR
SELF-PORTRAIT
1780S
Black and white chalk
Victoria and Albert Museum, London/De Agostini/ Bridgeman Images

Known to confidently defy convention, this self-portrait is disarmingly vulnerable. The close crop of the image and strong use of highlights draws particular attention to the wide eyes and clenched hands of the pose.

Think about how you can convey feeling through light.
Just a dash of highlight or shadow can completely
change the mood of a subject's face.

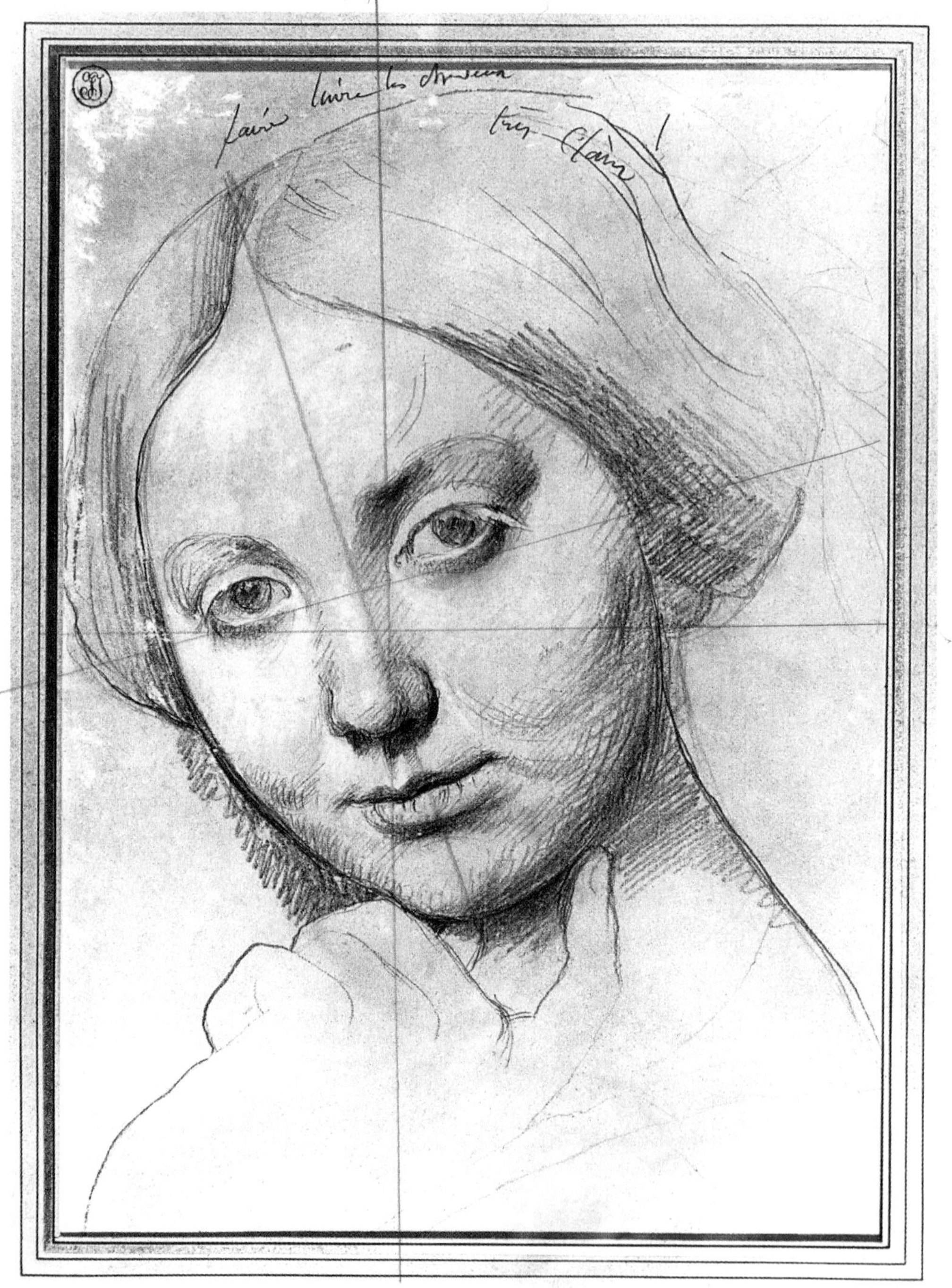

Jean-Auguste-Dominique Ingres
(1780–1867)
LOUISE DE BROGLIE COUNTESS OF HAUSSONVILLE
C.1842
Graphite on paper
Musée Duplessis, Carpentras/ Bridgeman Images

The mouth is also riddled with a complex interweaving of folds, curves, flats, and lost-and-found edges. These nuances are needed by a perceptive person who might try to understand human nature.

ROBERT GENN

There is no symmetry in nature. One eye is never like the other; it's different.
No one has a perfect nose, the mouth is always irregular.
ÉDOUARD MANET

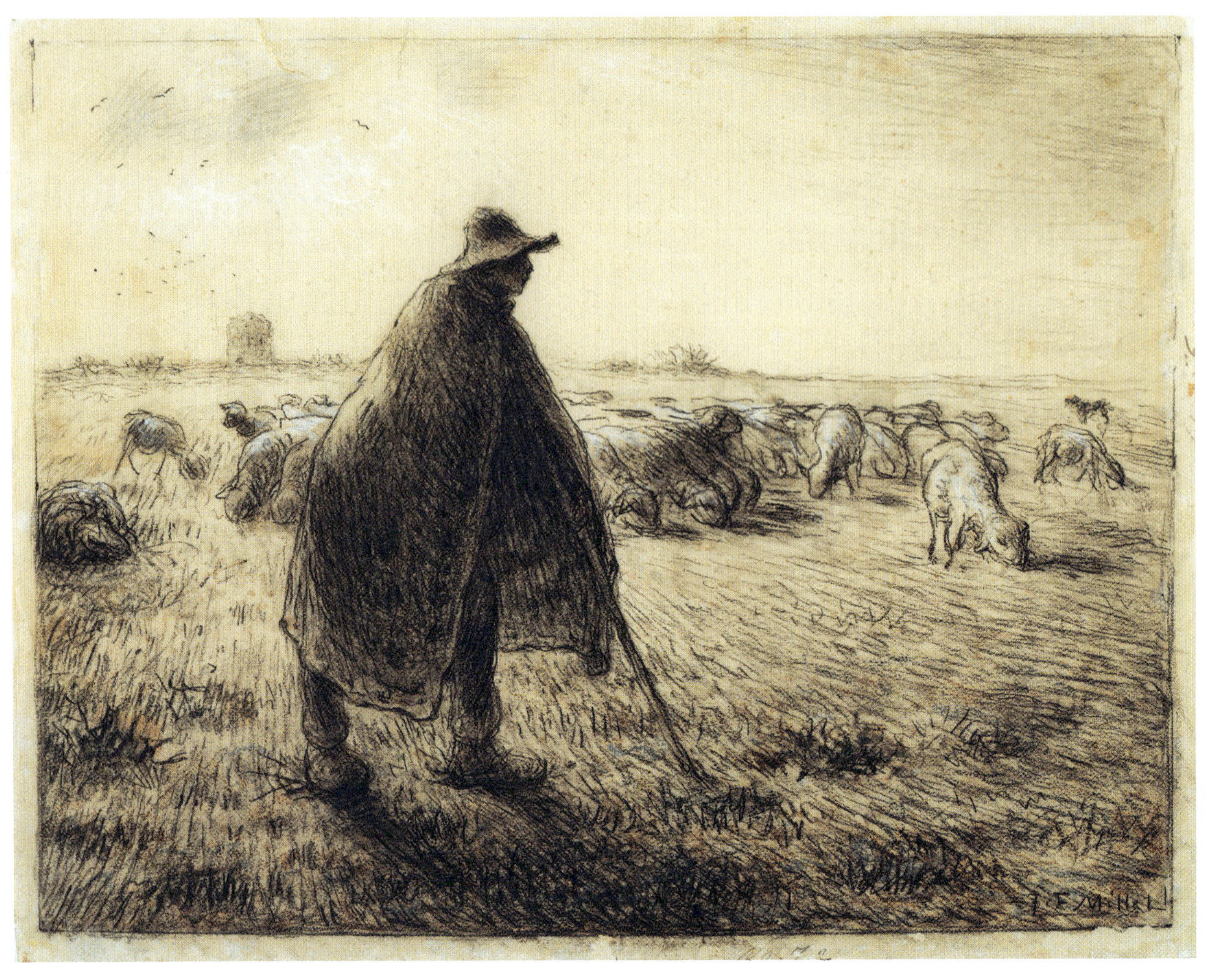

Jean-François Millet

(1814–75)

THE SHEPHERD

C.1872–4

Conté crayon on paper

The Phillips Collection, Washington, DC/ Bridgeman Images

Conté crayon is very difficult to erase, not allowing for mistakes or rather forcing the artist to focus and embrace the medium's limitations. Challenge yourself by putting your eraser away and taking your time to place each mark.

All art is but dirtying the paper delicately.

JOHN RUSKIN

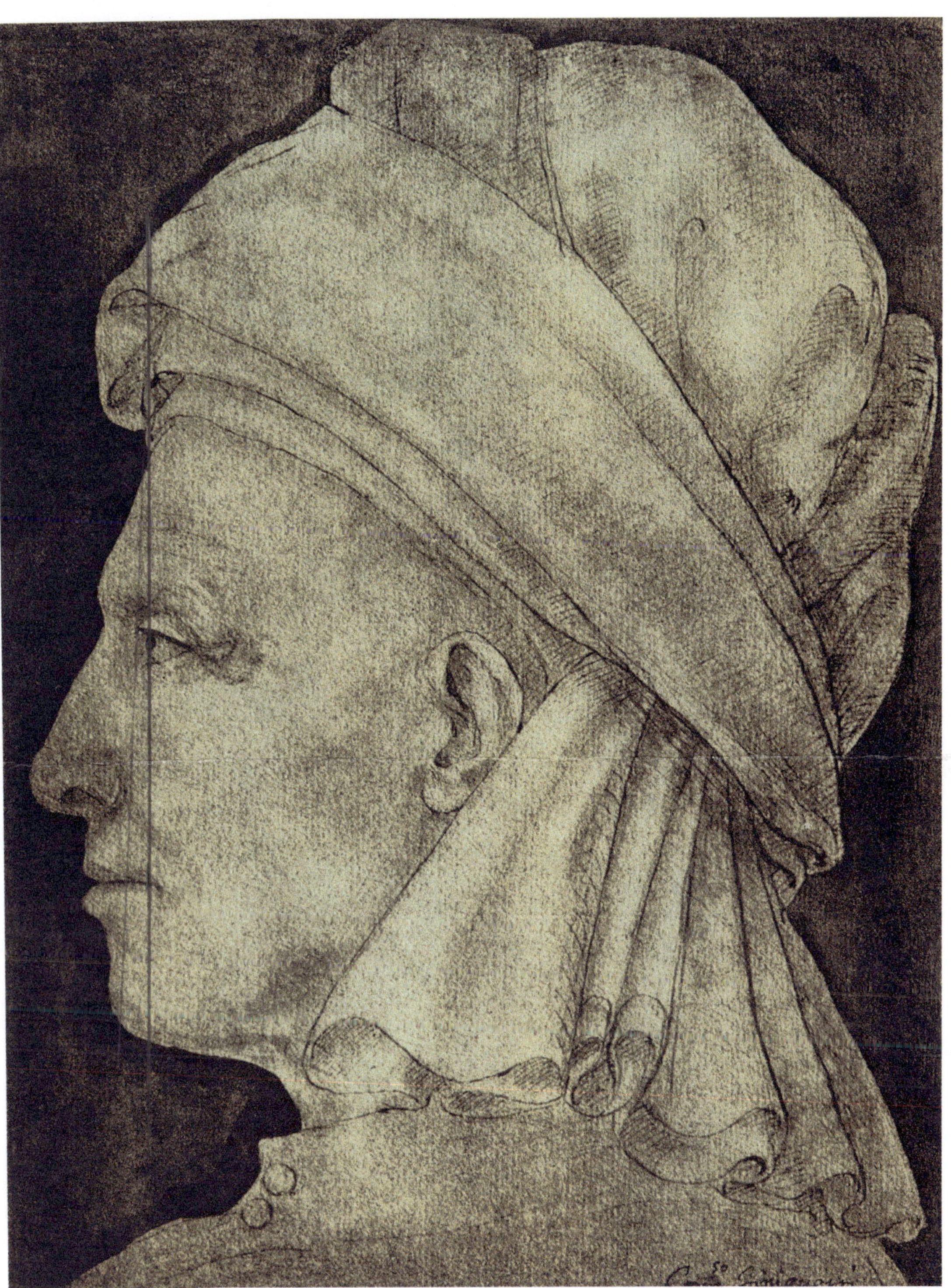

Paolo Uccello
(1397–1475)
DRAWING OF A
MAN'S PROFILE
15TH CENTURY
Alinari Archives/Corbis via Getty Images

—— *Portraits*

Since the cave paintings of prehistoric times, our first instinct as human beings has been to record our own image. As we are hardwired to recognize and respond to the human form, the face and body continues to be a recurring theme throughout art history. Today, in an era of mass media and the Internet, where images can be shared globally in an instant, and in a world in which we are routinely recorded via CCTV and constantly record ourselves through selfies, the desire for distinctive, thoughtful portraiture still endures.

Drawing can be a dynamic part of preparing a composition: acting as the visual armature that lies beneath a painting or the study that precedes a sculpture. However, drawing should also be valued as an end in itself—all the more pleasing for its immediacy and freedom of expression. This sketchbook is part of a series to help develop your drawing across different subjects, and in this book, we present a selection of portraits to show a range of portraiture styles through the ages, to copy from and be inspired by. There are also thoughts by commentators and the artists themselves, and a general information section is included on materials and techniques for the beginner.

You don't have to wait until you have the time to create a full portrait; preparatory sketches, practice exercises, or even a few scribbles will go a long way to sharpening your observational skills. Leonardo da Vinci (1452–1519) advised his fellow artists to be constantly alert to the world around them and always carry a sketchbook: "Make a note . . . with a few lines in your little book which you should always take with you . . . [and keep these] sketches as your aids and teachers." In time, this sketchbook will become a record of your progress and commitment to honing your skills.

Although you could concentrate initially on proportions, and making accurate copies of the example portraits, you will be able to broaden your knowledge with a host of other skills: mark-making, rendering basic forms, showing light and dark, and a better understanding of anatomy, foreshortening, and perspective. The aim of this book is to inspire you to express your own interpretations of portraits that are full of personality by developing your techniques in a genre that continues to intrigue, engage, and challenge.

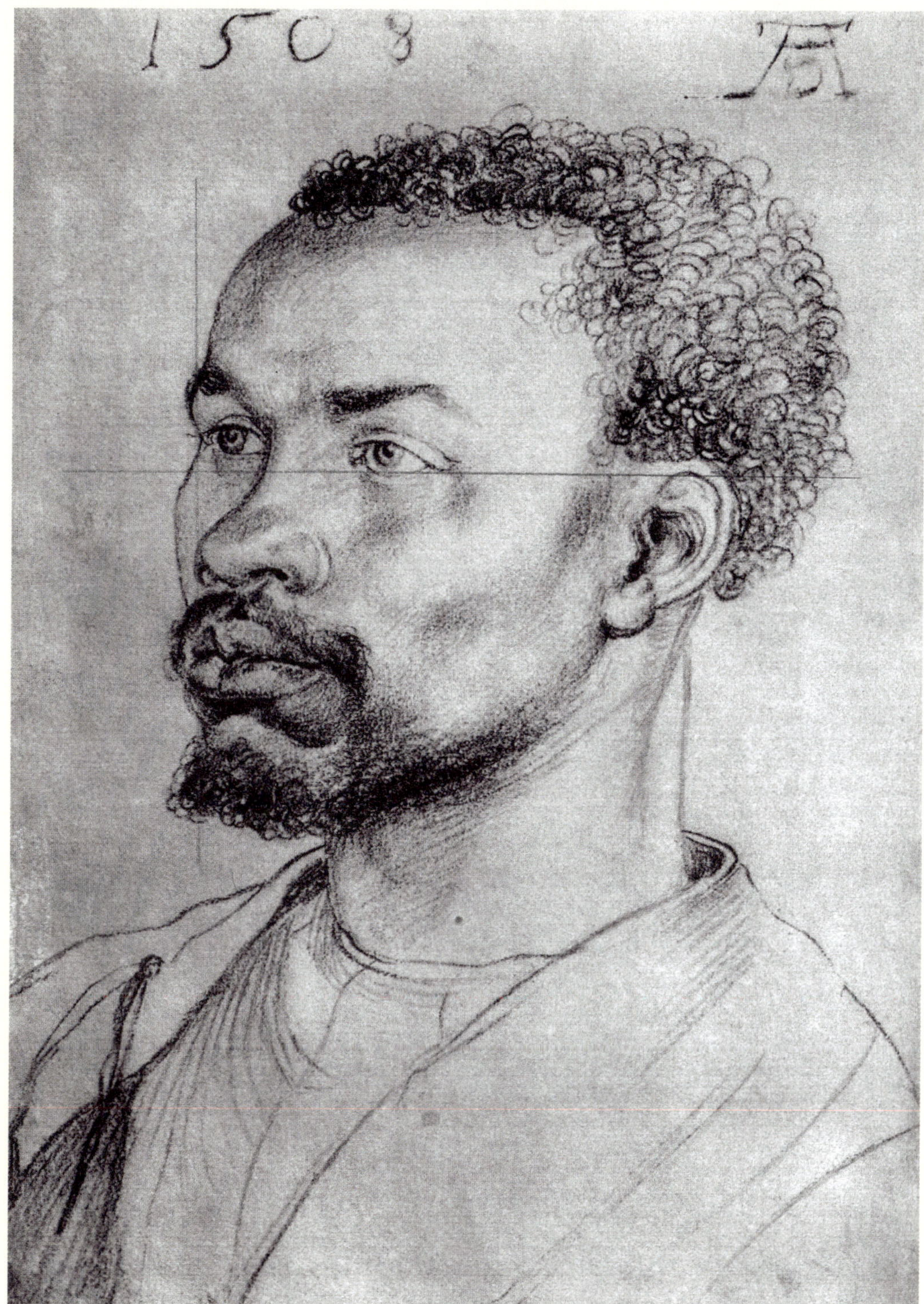

Albrecht Dürer
(1471–1528)
HEAD OF AN
AFRICAN
1508
Black chalk
Print Collector/Getty Images

Edgar Degas
(1834–1917)
MISS LALA AT THE FERNANDO CIRCUS (MISS LALA AT THE CIRQUE FERNANDO)
1879
Pastel
J. Paul Getty Museum, Los Angeles

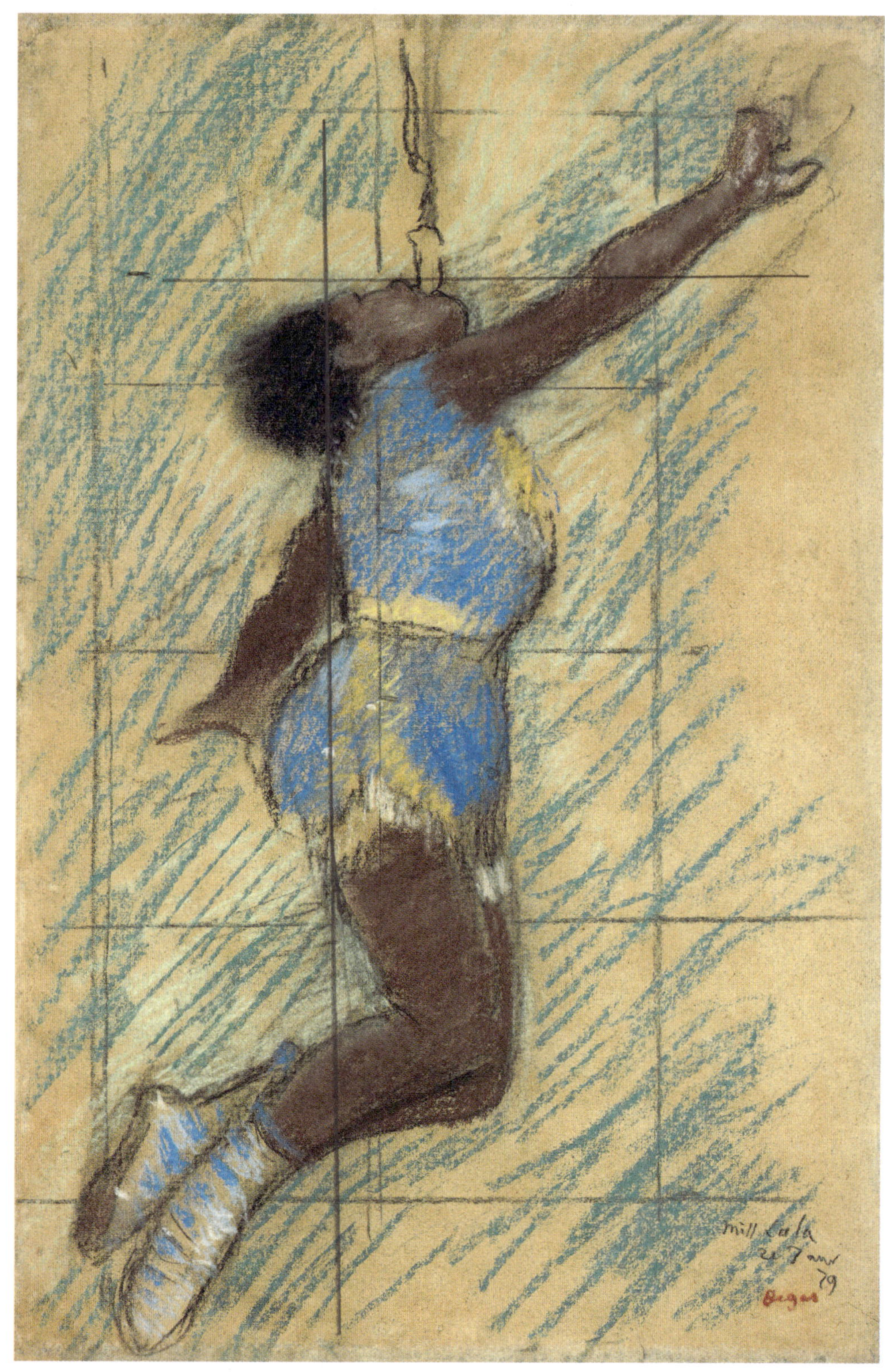

By means of a back, we want a temperament, an age, a social condition, to be revealed; through a pair of hands, we should be able to express a magistrate or a tradesman; by a gesture, a whole series of feelings.

EDGAR DEGAS

Art is not what you see, but what you make others see.

EDGAR DEGAS

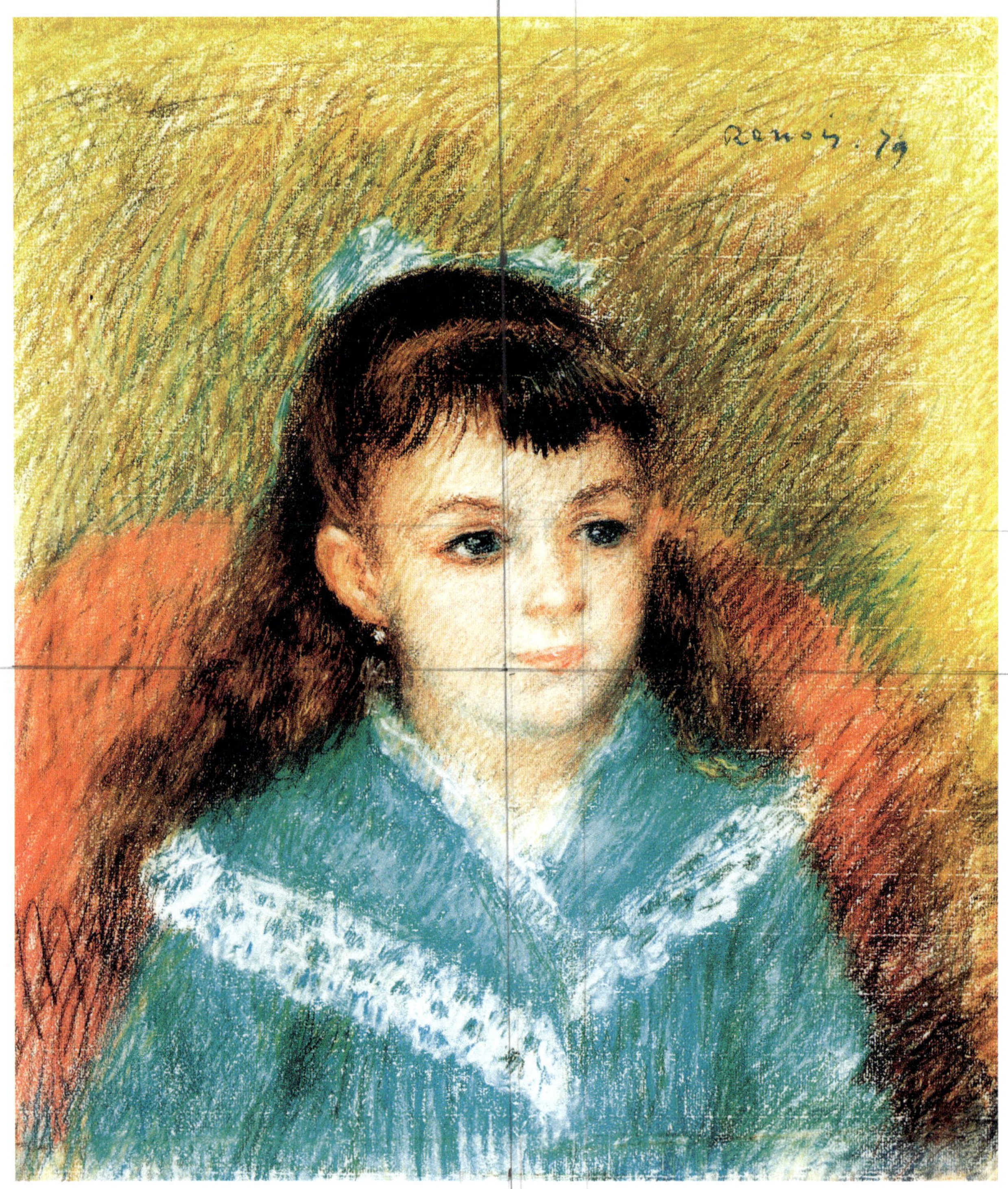

Pierre-Auguste Renoir
(1841–1919)
PORTRAIT OF A YOUNG GIRL
1879
Pastel on paper
Archivart/Alamy Stock Photo

A work might raise questions about the sitter's personality or connection with the artist. Here the six-year-old Elisabeth Maître wears a beautifully intriguing expression—is it amusement? Shyness? How can you capture the personality and uniqueness of your sitter in your work?

Nothing in a portrait is a matter of indifference. Gesture, grimace, clothing, decor even—all must combine to realize a character.

CHARLES BAUDELAIRE

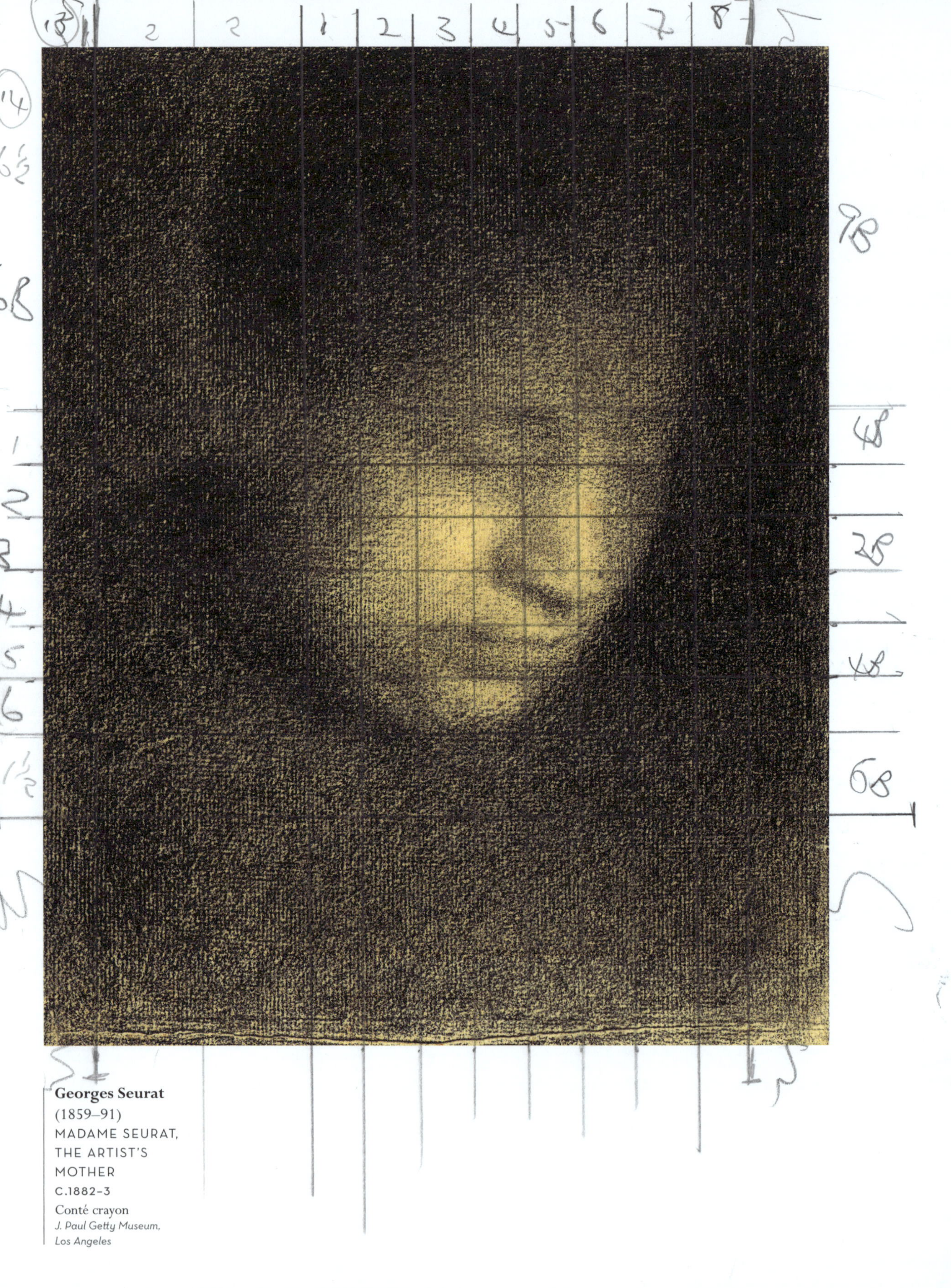

Georges Seurat
(1859–91)
MADAME SEURAT, THE ARTIST'S MOTHER
C.1882–3
Conté crayon
J. Paul Getty Museum, Los Angeles

Seurat has suggested the ghostlike form of his mother's face by building up modulated layers of conté crayon on textured stock, leaving only the places where the white paper shows through to reveal her features. Almost no lines are used in this composition.

Everything that you can see, in the world around you, presents itself to your eyes only as an arrangement of patches of different colors variously shaded.

JOHN RUSKIN

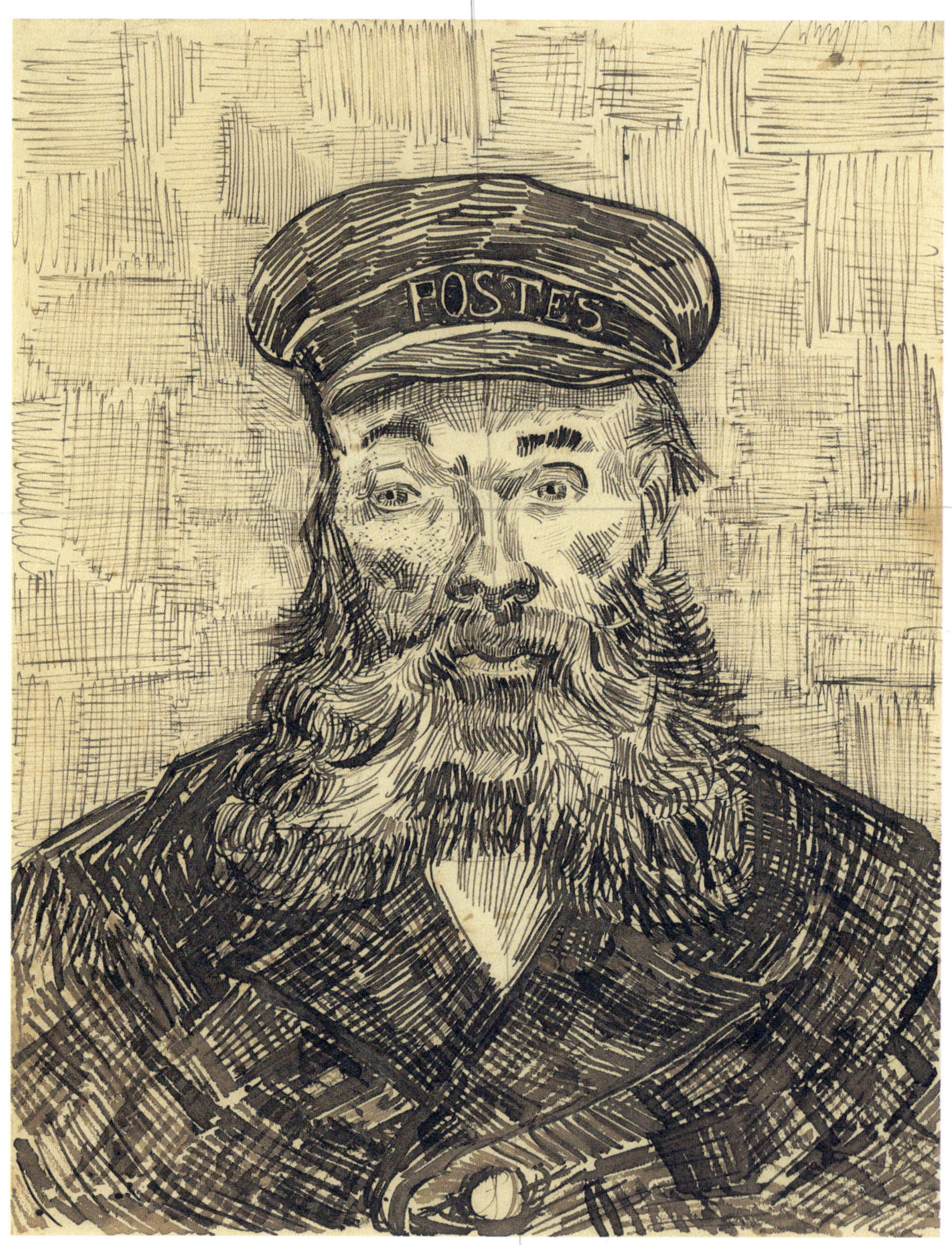

Vincent van Gogh
(1853–90)
PORTRAIT OF
JOSEPH ROULIN
1888
Reed and quill pen
and brown ink, over
black chalk
J. Paul Getty Museum,
Los Angeles

This moving portrait of van Gogh's friend, a postal worker, is made up of thousands of lines. Shadow and texture are convincingly communicated through the simple, dynamic techniques of hatching and crosshatching.

It constantly remains a source of disappointment to me that my drawings are not yet what I want them to be. The difficulties are indeed numerous and great . . . but as one stands before such a task, the basic necessities are patience and faithfulness.

VINCENT VAN GOGH

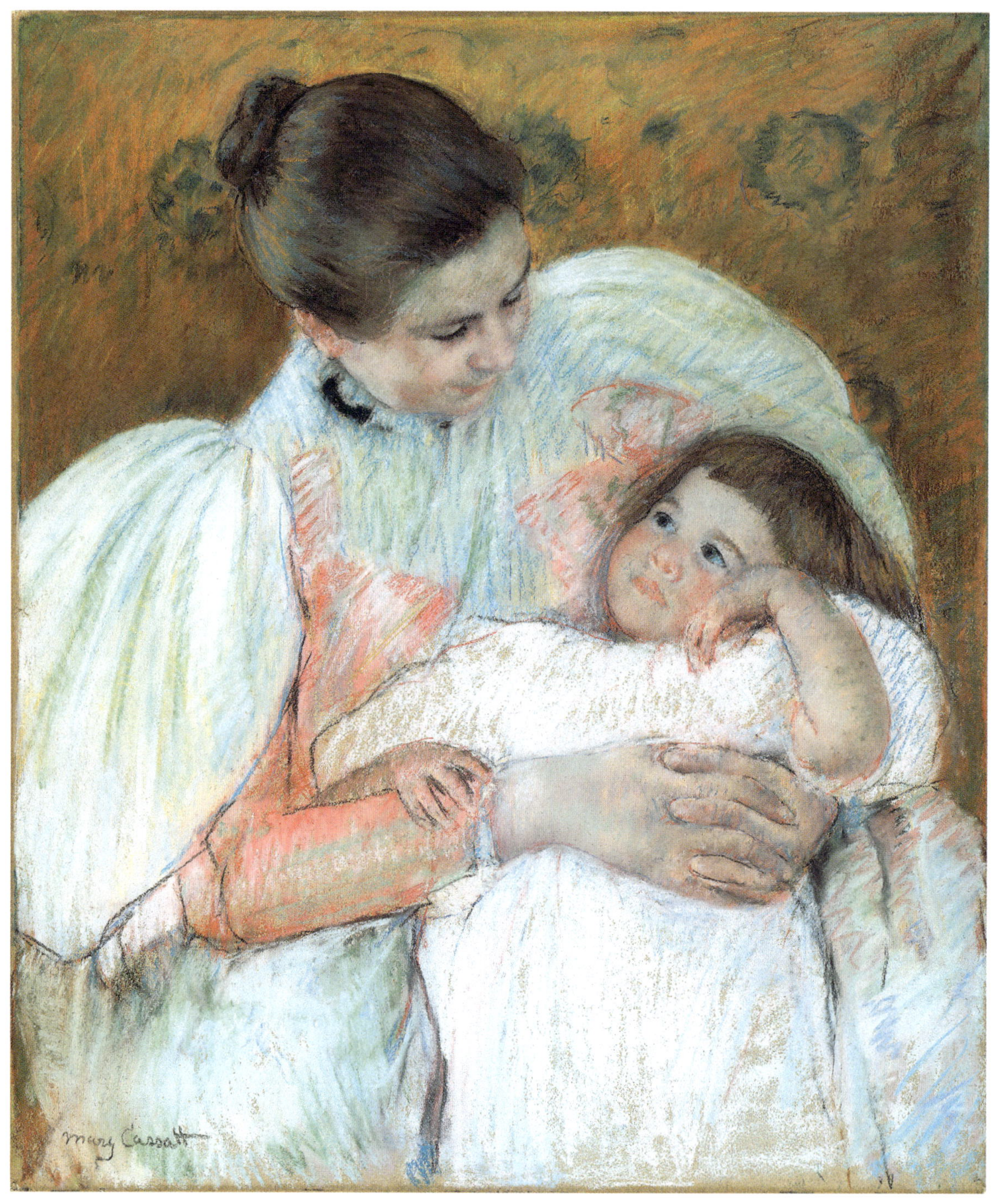

Mary Cassatt
(1844–1926)
NURSE AND CHILD
1896–7
Pastel on wove paper (originally blue), mounted on canvas
The Metropolitan Museum of Art/Art Resource/ Photo Scala, Florence

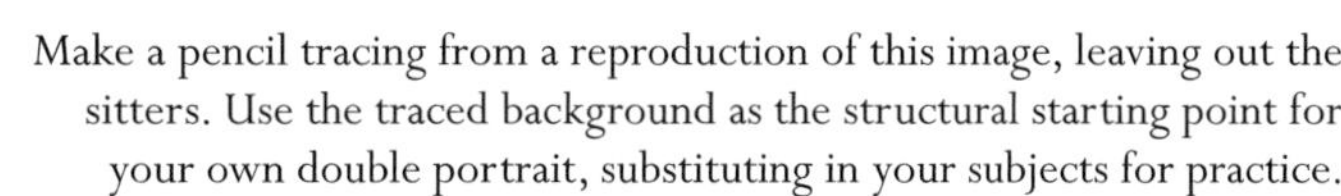

Make a pencil tracing from a reproduction of this image, leaving out the sitters. Use the traced background as the structural starting point for your own double portrait, substituting in your subjects for practice.

If I take a sheet of paper of given dimensions I will jot down a drawing which will have a necessary relation to its format . . . a drawing must have a power of expansion which can bring to life the space which surrounds it.

HENRI MATISSE

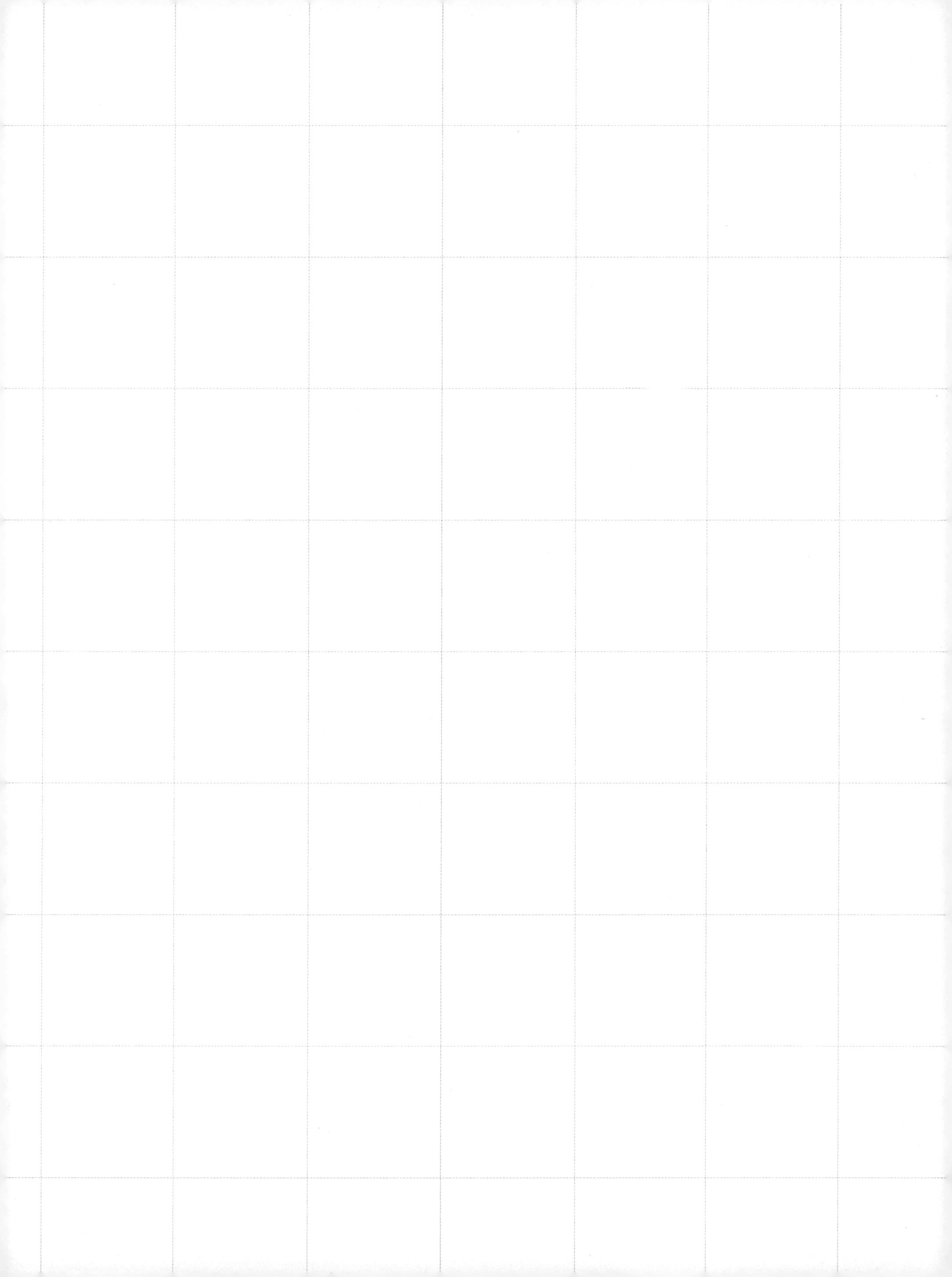

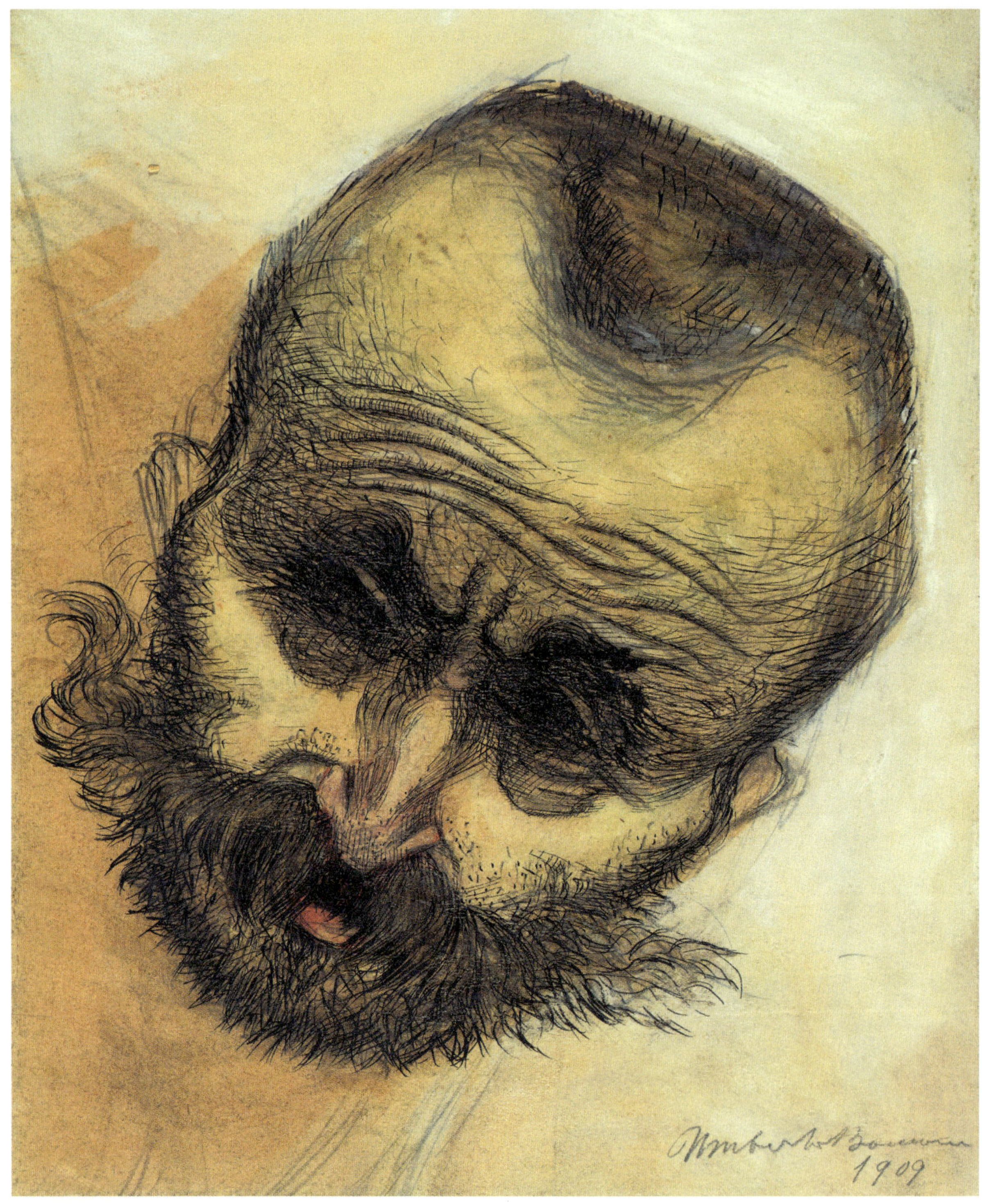

Umberto Boccioni
(1882–1916)
HEAD STUDY
1909
Pen and ink wash
The Leicester Galleries, London/Bridgeman Images

A portrait, in order to be a work of art, must not resemble the sitter . . . you must render its surrounding atmosphere.

UMBERTO BOCCIONI

To draw hair and facial hair, don't think so much in terms of individual hairs, but about the collective outline shapes they form. You can then build up the texture to show the style of the hair.

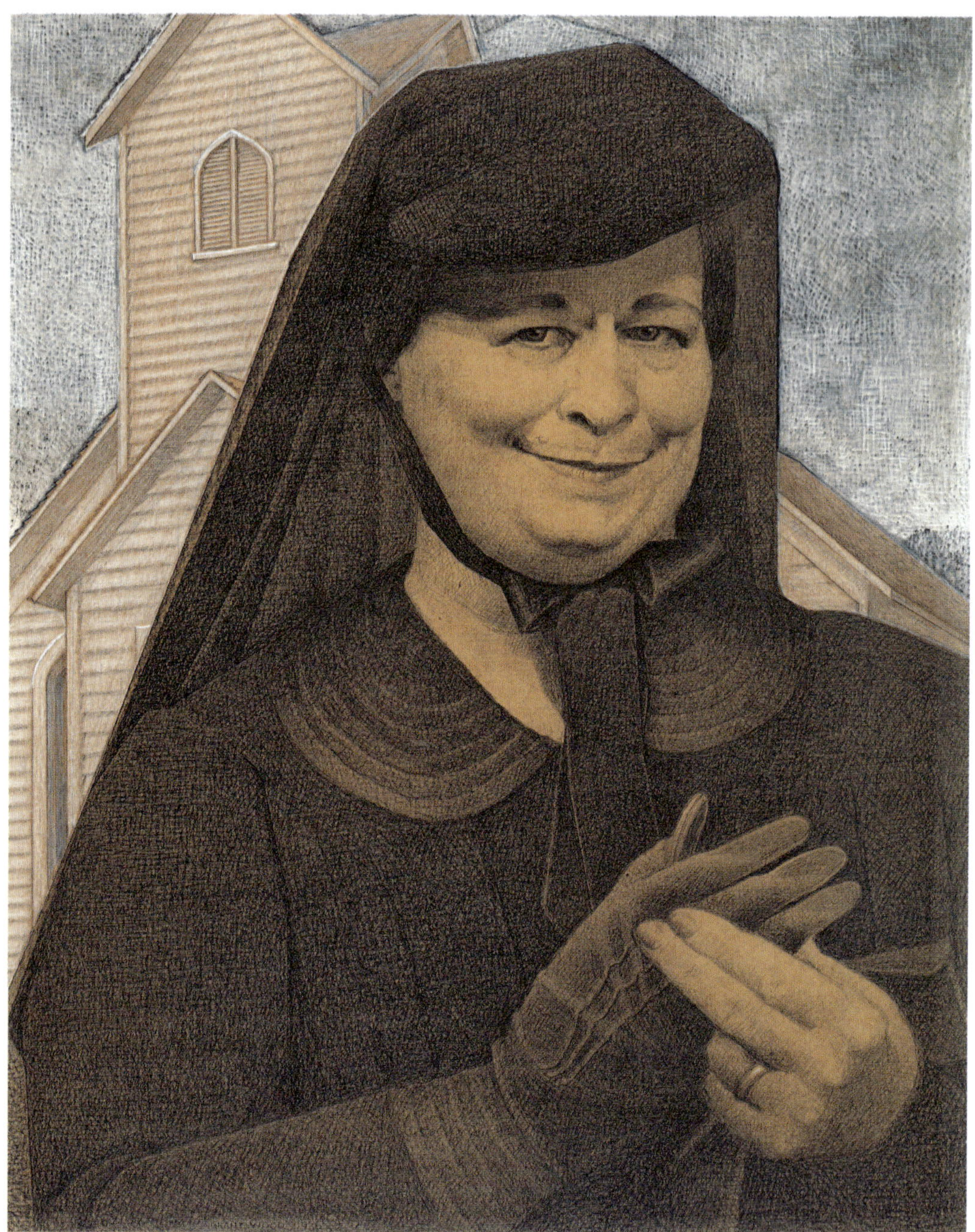

Grant Wood
(1891–1942)
THE GOOD INFLUENCE
1936
Black carbon pencil, India ink, and white gouache on tan wove paper
Courtesy of the Pennsylvania Academy of the Fine Arts, Philadelphia. Collections Fund

Is this a portrait of a person or a nation? The sitter's old-fashioned dress and the iconic architecture behind offer an archaic vision of the midwestern, American heartland—serving as a romantic ideal and an eerie time capsule.

Wood promoted an imagined rural landscape populated with recognizable stereotypes—the people in his art serve more as props than subjects. Consider how you might use your sitter to communicate a concept. Dress, setting, expression, and gesture will help the viewer read the sitter.

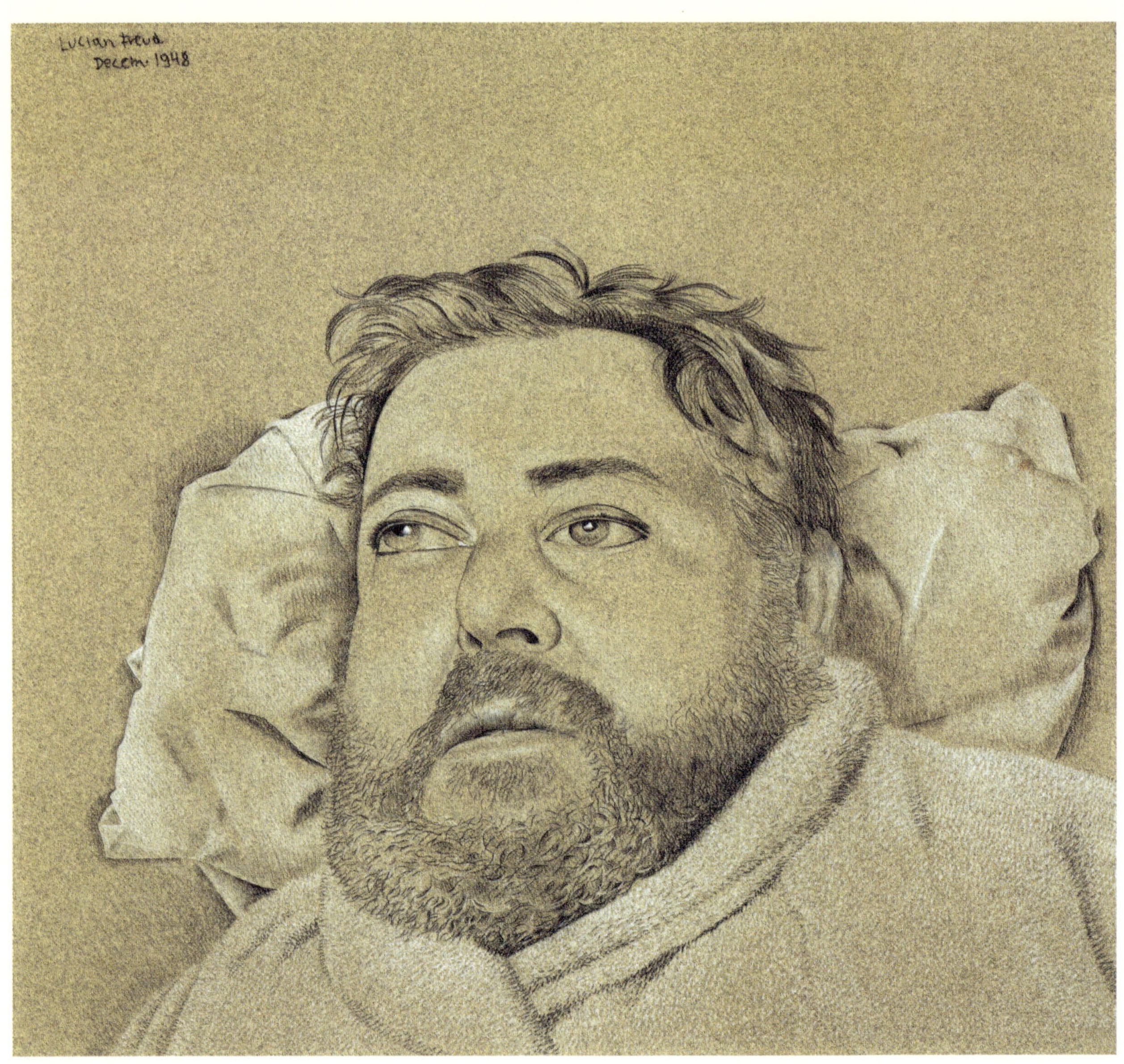

Lucian Freud
(1922–2011)
CHRISTIAN BÉRARD
1948
Black and white
conté pencil on buff
Ingres paper
Private Collection/
Bridgeman Images

In this intimate yet confrontational work, Freud's sitter raises his head upward and toward the viewer as if nose to nose. The close-up perspective magnifies Bérard's features, allowing for serious scrutiny and drawing the viewer in ever closer.

Freud tells more that is to his purpose and ours on the frequent occasions when he loses himself altogether in someone else. Such was the occasion on which he drew . . . the head of Christian Bérard, ailing and querulous yet immense in his authority, a Czar of style.

LAWRENCE GOWING

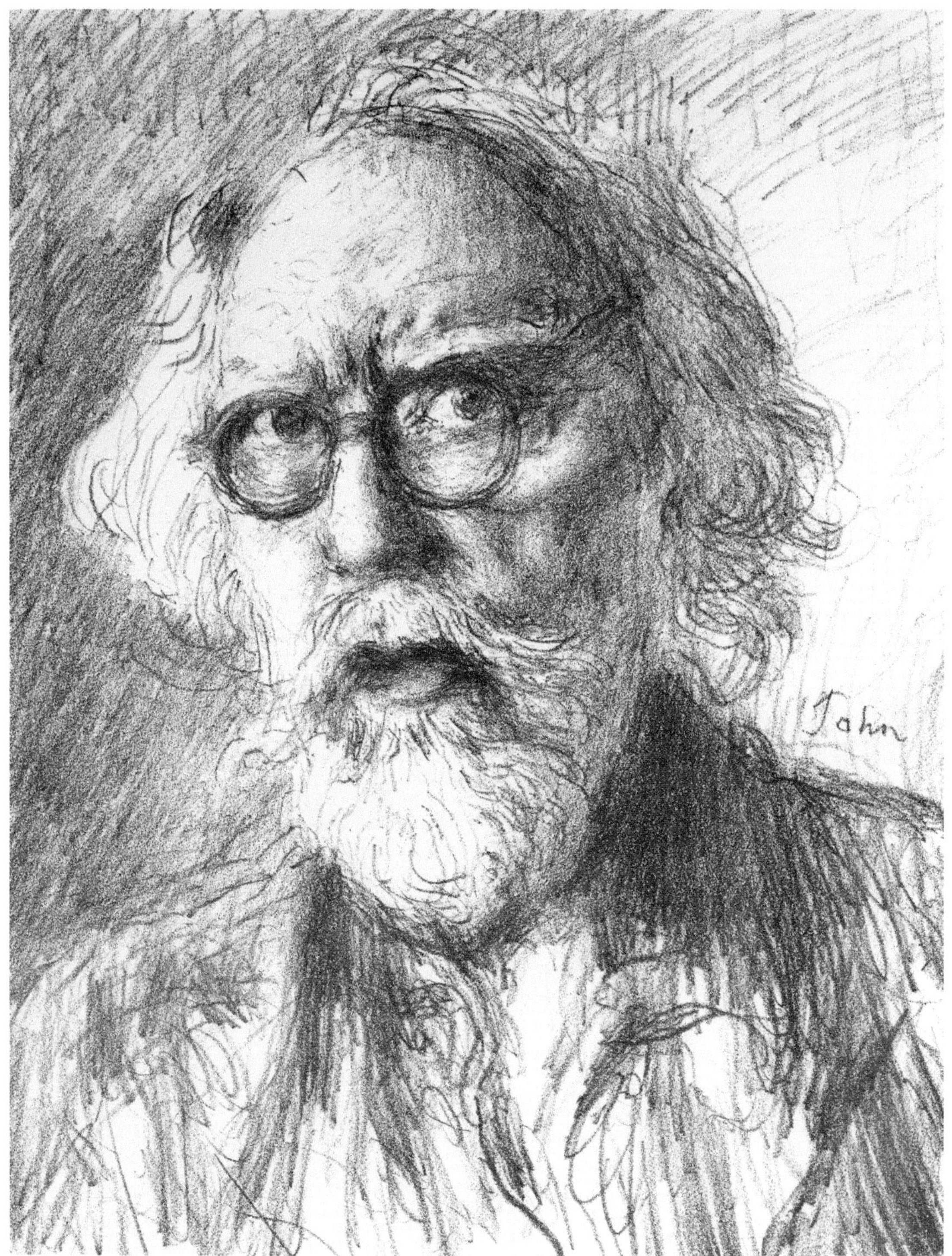

Augustus John
(1878–1961)
SELF PORTRAIT
1956
Pencil
Private Collection/
Bridgeman Images

Self-portraiture is a singular in-turned art. Something eerie lurks in its fingering of the edge between seer and seen.

JULIAN BELL

Treat spectacles as you might the eyes, ears, nose, or any other part of the face. Do they have a shadow? How do they affect the rest of the face? Draw faithfully.

Pablo Picasso
(1881–1973),
1959, FROM 2ND BOOK IN *TOROS Y TOREROS*, PUBLISHED BY LE CERCLE D'ART IN 1961
1959
Pen and ink and colored crayon
Private Collection/Bridgeman Images © Succession Picasso, DACS, London 2017

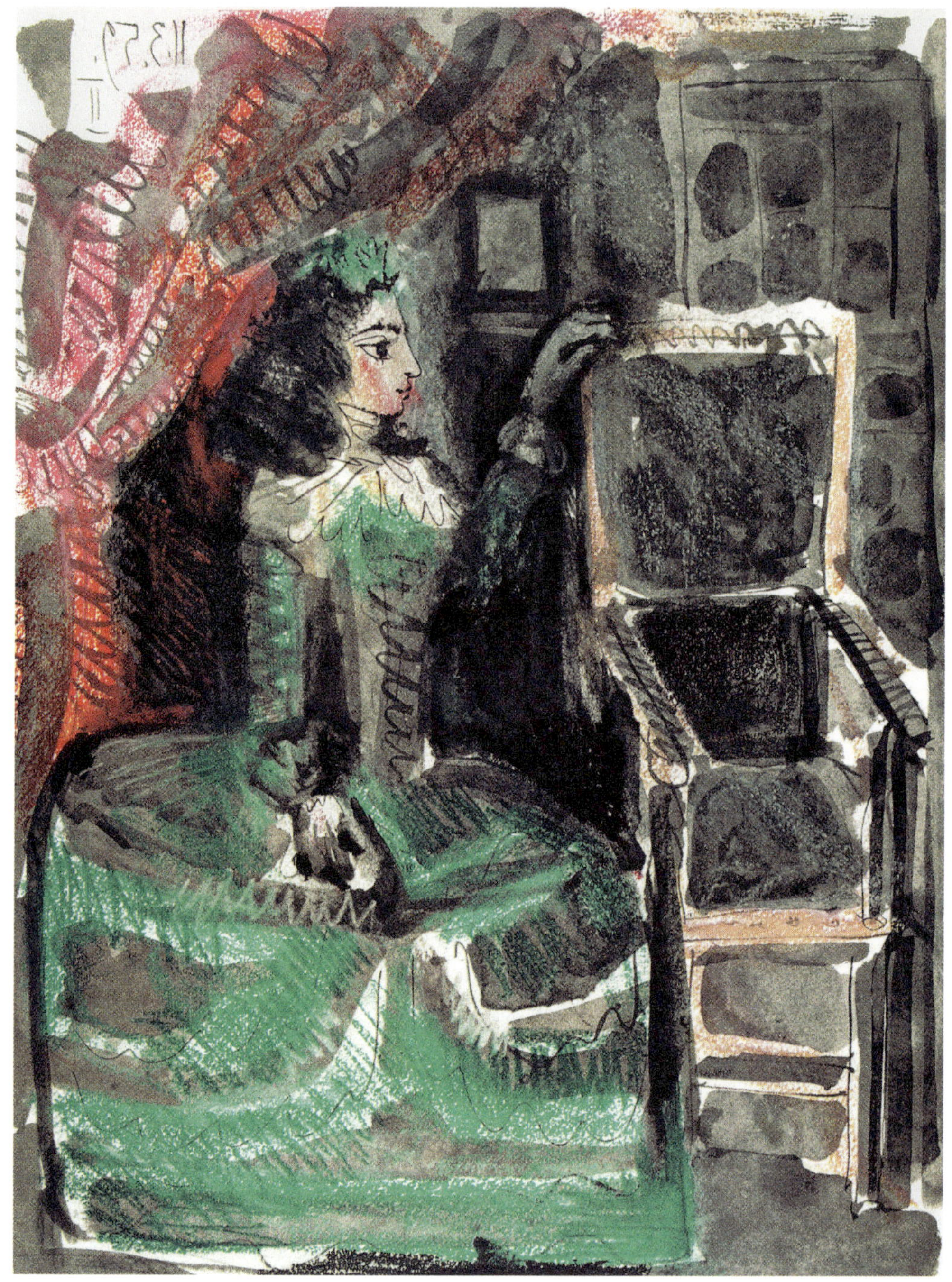

Create a portrait imitating the style of an artist you like, imagining how that artist would approach your subject. Then re-create the portrait in a style that is distinctly your own.

All I have tried to do is to derive, from a complete knowledge of tradition, a reasoned sense of my own independence and individuality.

GUSTAVE COURBET

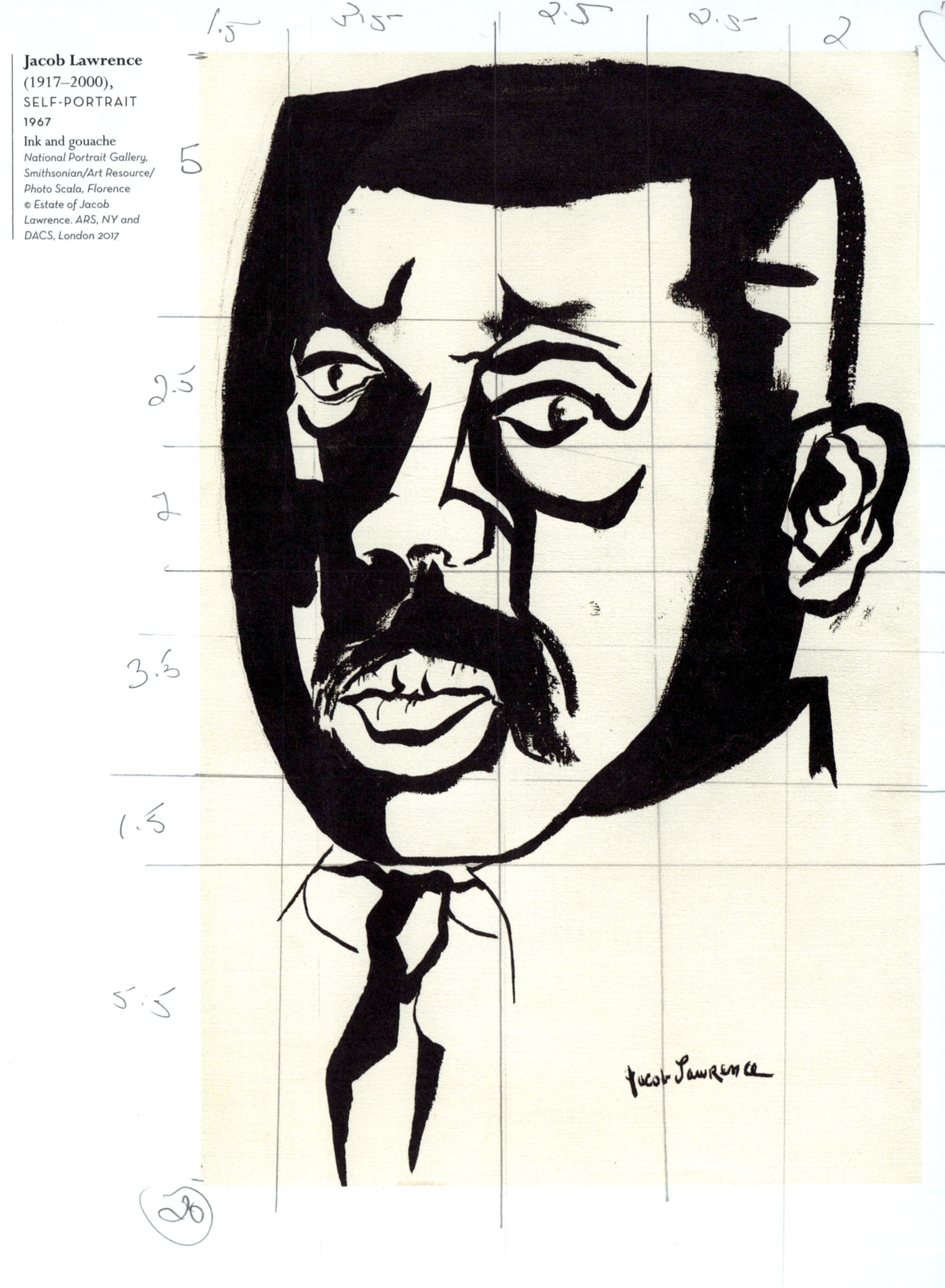

Jacob Lawrence (1917–2000), SELF-PORTRAIT
1967
Ink and gouache
National Portrait Gallery, Smithsonian/Art Resource/Photo Scala, Florence © Estate of Jacob Lawrence. ARS, NY and DACS, London 2017